PRINCESS VEASLEY

A JOURNEY
TO
FREEDOM
AND
PURPOSE

Her Voice

*Get Your Voice Back and Embrace Your
Healing Journey After Heartbreak and Betrayal*

If you would like to purchase bulk copies of Her Voice, please contact us at hello@whosheis.com for discounted pricing.

1st edition, November 2024

ISBN-13	: 979-8-218-52821-8

To Paris, Paytin, and Paisley

May you always remember that life is more than you can see now. Focus on the only one who can truly give your life meaning and purpose.

I love you always.

Contents

Introduction

Without her voice, she will never be able to become the woman God created her to be. Her purpose and destiny are put on hold as she runs in a perpetual cycle to keep her distracted from reaching the point of fully surrendering her plans for God's plan. The enemy knows that as long as he can keep her bound by relationships and bad choices, he has nothing to worry about because she will never become who she is destined to be. It's time to step into who God created you to be and live a life of freedom without compromising your faith in God for the sake of relationships or anything else this life brings.

Part One

Hey girl, let's grow.

Chapter 1

HER WORTH

"She is more precious than rubies."

I never thought about my worth as a woman until I was asked a very specific question. I didn't know it then, but this question stuck with me for the rest of my life. "How much do you value yourself as a woman?" the counselor at the mental hospital asked me. During this season of my life, I was married and dealing with a lot of emotional trauma. I didn't want to end my marriage because I believed things would eventually change. I was married young, and I had formed my identity around my relationship. I didn't know who I was; I couldn't tell you what I liked, loved, or even enjoyed, for that matter. I liked whatever my husband liked and lost my sense of being an individual.

This didn't just start after marriage. It began in my teenage years. I was raised to know Christ and was taught the Word Of God, but I still didn't understand who I was in Christ. I had morals and beliefs, but how I saw myself was skewed. I felt like I needed someone to guide me, protect me, and show me the world, but I didn't realize I was searching for it in the wrong place.

"How much do you value yourself as a woman?"

I started dating seriously around 14/15 years old (because you know anything before that doesn't really count) and I would like to say that I started off okay. I had dated someone for 3 years, and I thought I was in love; I mean, I just knew we were going to get married after college. It wasn't until the topic of sex came up that ended the relationship. I was determined to save myself for marriage, but this wasn't mutual. I was hurt, but I became determined to prove that I didn't need him and could find someone better. However, once I adopted this mindset, I didn't realize I was only working against myself. What I once believed to be sacred for marriage led me into experiences that ultimately changed the entire course of my life.

You may be wondering how I ended up in a mental hospital because I definitely didn't believe I should have been there. But, because of a misunderstanding on my part, I was stuck there for a few days. The crazy thing is God knew exactly what I needed, and the time I spent trapped there wasn't wasted.

It was a Sunday afternoon, and I found myself being questioned by my husband, at the time, about whether I had been talking to anyone while we were dating or during the marriage. He couldn't believe that I had been faithful to him since we had started dating back in 2005. After he kept bringing it up repeatedly, I finally broke down and admitted to him that I had a male friend whom I would talk to from time to time. I told him that whenever I felt he was out messing around on me, I would talk to him. We were friends before I met my ex-husband and we would hang out in the car, usually parked outside his house, and talk about whatever came to mind. However, once we got engaged, I ended the friendship, and I didn't speak to him again, that is until this day came around. After sharing this with my ex-husband, things escalated quickly, and he threatened to leave me. I couldn't believe he was taking it this far; I mean, he had me look him up on Facebook to talk to him and everything. Even though I hadn't talked to him in years, I complied because I didn't have anything to hide. I called my old friend on the phone and asked him exactly what my ex-husband told me to ask: "Did we have sex?"

So pause. This was a super awkward situation to be in because this man was absolutely clueless as to what was going on, and on top of that, I felt embarrassed because now he knew that there was trouble in paradise.

After repeating the question again, confused, he answered as I thought he would and said, "NO, why would you ask me that?". But even after this, it still wasn't enough. "I'm done with you" are the words I felt I heard coming out of my ex-husband's mouth. At this point, I didn't know what to do but make a scene. Isn't that what we all do when things don't go our way? Next thing you know I'm in tears, running to the car yelling, "YOU CAN SEE ME AT MY FUNERAL!" and I sped off dramatically. You know, it's funny as I reflect back on this now, but at that moment, my emotions were all over the place. I didn't know what to do. As I entered the highway, I began to think about what had happened. I said to myself, "I'm not about to kill myself; I'm going to go back home, get the girls, and go to the park for a while to cool off". But to my surprise, when I arrived, the police were there, directing me to pull further down the street to talk to me. He asked me how I was feeling, and I responded truthfully but with a little extra because, you know, when you are highly emotional, you can tend to overreact just a little. "Not good", I responded. "If I had a gun, I would shoot myself." *Now, I don't know why in the world I said this to an officer out of all people, but I did.* He then proceeded to ask me if I wanted to talk to someone, and I thought to myself that it would probably be better than staying here, so I said yes.

Next thing you know, I was sitting in a waiting room, which led to another waiting room, which led to another, and finally to a room that looked like a common area but with a nurses station and rooms around the perimeter. I sat on the couch thinking, what kind of a counseling office is this?! I started to notice the people in the room, and I became confused as to what was happening. So I did what anyone would do and decided to ask one of the nurses when I would be able to leave. I wasn't ready for the response because what I thought was going to be a couple of hours turned into a few days. That lady told me that I couldn't leave until I spoke with a doctor and that he would not be here until tomorrow. At this point, I was panicking because I had to go to work and take the kids to school, and the list went on. I didn't know what to do, so I asked to use the phone. I called my boss and let her know what was going on. I mean, I was stuck in this place and didn't know when I could get out. I remember sitting there hearing screams coming from another side of the building and seeing people there who dealt with issues from anger management to detoxing from drugs. After hearing why people were in this place, I knew I didn't belong here. I was in a psychiatric ward and all I could think of was that this was crazy! The next day came, and I finally got to talk to a counselor (which is what I thought I was going to do this entire time, but hey, it was better late than never).

I began to tell her what happened and what I blurted out to my husband about meeting me at my funeral. She then said, "When you say anything threatening to take your life, we are trained and held accountable for what you do next. That includes law enforcement, counselors, etc." She also said, "We must report and take what you said seriously." Then she asked me about my marriage, and I shared that during the ten years we were together, I couldn't recall one year that he was faithful to me. That's when she asked the life-changing question: "How do you value yourself as a woman?" And then it hit me. I didn't value myself at all. I had been in a relationship that had proven to be unhealthy, and I continued to put myself in situations that consequently broke me.

How often do we betray ourselves for the sake of keeping a relationship? How long will we ignore the voice in our head to leave or to end it? We tell ourselves that it's going to get better, that it will change, and that the love will come, only to find ourselves broken

> *How often do we betray ourselves for the sake of keeping a relationship?*

and lost. This was me, but God knew exactly what I needed in that season of life. Who knew that going to a mental hospital would be the very thing to open my eyes and help me evaluate my life? I was there for a few days; I couldn't leave and had to follow a tight schedule. I couldn't just do whatever I wanted, but this ultimately gave me time away from my reality at home. The time I spent there was just long enough for me to understand that this was not where I needed to be in life.

> *"I praise you because I am fearfully and wonderfully made; your works are wonderful, I know that full well."*
>
> Psalms 139 : 14 NIV

Knowing your worth begins with understanding who you are in Christ Jesus because, without this knowledge, your identity and vision will become skewed. You will look to others and allow them to tell you who you are while forgetting that God has already done that job. You may have been hurt, betrayed, abused, or overlooked, but don't allow the enemy to stand in the way of the true authority you have. Understand that coming to know Christ, what he did for you, and how you're a daughter of the King is game-changing. You are of a royal priesthood because you already have citizenship in Heaven! You are fearfully and wonderfully made, so beautiful and complex. If only you knew that you were created to tread across serpents and flourish in the calling that God has created for you, maybe you would see yourself differently. You are a princess to God. You are His daughter. Ask God to change the way you see yourself and the way you see Him. Know that you have been forgiven, and nothing can separate you from the love of God. You are not your mistakes, nor are you your past. You can no longer afford to subject yourself to situations and people who were meant to keep you stagnant, crippled, and defeated. It's time to rise to the occasion and take your rightful place as a daughter of the King.

I have given you authority to trample on snakes and scorpions and to overcome all the power of the enemy; nothing will harm you.

Luke 10:19 NIV

Chapter 2

HER IDENTITY

"She knows who she is."

I found that your identity in Christ will often be attacked at a young age, and it starts in the mind. If the enemy can convince you to believe that your sin is too great for God to forgive or cause you to believe a lie and mask who you are, then you'll eventually receive the curses of confusion and mental attacks. You will start to seek validation from people instead of God. You'll begin to compare yourself to others and become insecure. You'll begin to desire acceptance from people and relationships, which ultimately leaves you desperate, depressed, and vulnerable - trying to prove your worth or worthiness. You will just go with the flow and follow people who don't even know where they are headed themselves. The devil knows that if he can keep you clueless about who you are in Christ, he will keep you bound.

I heard a story years ago about how people would train an elephant in a certain way to control them. When they were young, the caretakers would tie a rope on their feet to keep them from going wherever they wanted. As the elephants grew and became much bigger and stronger, they would still use that same rope to keep them bound. Even though the elephant could easily break free, it didn't because of how it was conditioned to think. The elephant didn't believe that it could be free because it remembered how hard it was when it was smaller, so it chose to stay bound.

Ephesians 4:27 NLT Says, *"Don't give a foothold to the devil"*. Although the scripture was used to talk about being angry, I find it quite useful in this way as well. Because all the enemy has to do is make you believe that you can't, to keep that "foothold" on you and limit how far you can go.

Knowing your identity in Christ is the key to growing in your walk with God and unlocking what God placed inside of you. The enemy knows this, too; that is why he will attempt to take you out before you can even get started. So, let's talk about your identity in Christ because, for the longest, I had a hard time understanding what that really means and what it looks like.

(Definition - Foothold: Opportunity, power, occasion for acting)

What is your identity in Christ?

Once you accept Jesus Christ as your Lord and Savior, you have been given a NEW identity that is in Christ. This identity comes with the benefits from the price he paid for you so that you can now be free from the wages and bondage of sin. You now identify as a child of God! Because you have been adopted into the royal family, you now have citizenship in heaven *(Philippians 3:20)*. It's a celebration, and you have been given the free gift of the Holy Spirit. *(Ephesians 1:13)* This gift is special because it is only given to those who belong to Christ. The Holy Spirit enables us to do what pleases God. *(Philippians 2:13)* Without him, it would be impossible. We are now a new person in Christ *(2 Corinthians 5:17)*, and because we are connected to the vine (Christ), we will bear much fruit. *(John 15:1-7)* Fruit means the fruits of the holy spirit.

This is how we are identified as one of God's Children. *(Matthew 7:16)* Because the Holy Spirit lives within us, our character will begin to display (love, joy, peace, patience, kindness, goodness, gentleness, faithfulness, and self-control.) *(Galatians 5:22-26)* This doesn't mean that we will be perfect, but we are made perfect in Christ. *(Hebrews 10:14)* And it is not by might nor by our power that we will be able to accomplish this. It is only by the Holy Spirit and its power working within us that we will be able to accomplish these things. *(Philippians 2:13)*

Our identity in Christ is simply becoming a Child of God

To recap, our identity in Christ is simply becoming a Child of God. Our character will begin to show that we are a Child of God because of the Holy Spirit living within us to help us do what pleases God and become who God has called us to be.

> *But the Holy Spirit produces this kind of fruit in our lives: love, joy, peace, patience, kindness, goodness, faithfulness, gentleness, and self-control. There is no law against these things!*
>
> Galatians 5:22 NLT

I encourage you to take some time to study the scriptures listed below. Talk to God and allow him to speak to you concerning the way he sees you. The most important position you can have with God is perfecting the office of a daughter. God says in his word that we should come to him as a child. *Matt. 18:3* Remember there is nothing that you've done that is too big for God to accept you as his own. God is waiting for you to come to him as you are and to allow him to mend your brokenness. You don't need to be perfect; you just need to be willing.

IDENTITY:

Psalm 139:15-16
Matthew 7:16
Romans 3:22, 3:24, 6:6, 8:1-2
Galatians 3:28, 4:26-29
Ephesians 1:5, 2:6, 2:10
Philippians 3:20
2 Corinthians 5:17
John 1:12-13

BLESSINGS & GIFTS:

Ephesians 1
Philippians 2:13
1 Corinthians 12
Galatians 5:22-26

Chapter 3

HER VISION & INFLUENCES

Becoming you

Our experiences will influence our perception in life. Just like a float drifting on the beach, if you are not careful, you will eventually look up and be in the middle of the ocean, trying to make your way back to shore. In the same sense, when things happen to us in our lives, the effects may seem small initially, but they tend to grow into bigger problems later in life.

The seed

Growing up in a two-parent household was normal for me. However, what I didn't know then is that just because you have both parents doesn't mean you're dealt the "perfect life hand" or that you'll grow up without "daddy issues". I was raised in the Lord, as I mentioned; however, the absence of my father affected me in ways I couldn't understand at the time. Although he was physically there, he was distant and disconnected the older I became. I naturally looked to him for guidance because he is my father, but when I needed it the most, he wasn't there. My dad is great, don't get me wrong; there were just moments that left an imprint on me as I grew in my adolescent years. At times, I felt afraid to ask him questions because he would get upset, and I didn't like that feeling. So, over time, I avoided it altogether. This mentally ended up following me into my relationships and eventually affected the way I would communicate with men. Here's the problem: when seeds are planted, we don't know who will come to water them. Furthermore, what starts off small typically grows into something much bigger. This is why, when going through the healing process, we have to identify the root of the problem and address it in order to successfully heal. (We will talk more about this in a later chapter). Because I was afraid of his reaction, I would avoid communicating, which can be unhealthy to a certain extent.

The watering

As I got older and began dating, I would look to more mature guys, thinking that they would be able to teach me about life and things I didn't know. I started dating someone who seemed to know it all and I looked to him as someone who could lead and protect me. However, I eventually discovered that he had anger management issues. Knowing that I already had the "fear of communicating with men" seed already planted inside me didn't help either. In fact, because I chose to stay in this relationship, the seed was watered and grew into insecurities. How was this possible? Well, when issues and concerns would arise, I found myself talking to him about it and he would blow up. He would make me feel like I didn't know what I was talking about and that he was always right. No matter how small the problems were, they always seemed to be a big issue with him. As a result, I felt inferior when it came to men as though I didn't know anything. I felt like I didn't know how to communicate with men because anytime I did, I would experience verbal abuse and belittling. I remember a time when I had upset him, and he walked up to my car and yelled at me as though he were a drill sergeant. I mean, his face was so close to mine that I could feel his breath and spit coming out of his mouth as he yelled profusely at me. At that moment I couldn't even speak and I didn't know what to say. I wasn't used to dealing with conflict in this way. Seeing what happened in this situation, the enemy used what was already planted in me to transform it into something that would ultimately silence my voice. I felt like nobody wanted to hear what I had to say. I didn't feel like I was important nor my thoughts. I was made to believe that everything I said was nonsense and I was always wrong.

Looking back on this journey, if I could speak to my younger self, I would say:

Princess, you are not inadequate. You are important, and your voice is important. Sometimes, people want to feel as though they know it all when really they don't. They won't admit when they are wrong because that would make them feel powerless. You don't have to prove yourself to people, and you shouldn't allow them to make you feel as though you're ignorant or misguided. Anyone who causes you to question yourself and doubt your ability to understand is playing a devious game called "manipulation". They want to feel a sense of control, so they will make sure they place themselves in the position of the "answer." Don't allow the enemy or people to silence your voice because that is what God has given you to use for the Kingdom. You made some poor decisions, but you don't have to stay in them. Let go of the people who don't value you and speak death instead of life. God did not create you to stay in toxic environments. It may not be easy, but it's time to go where you will flourish.

Don't allow the enemy or people to silence your voice because that is what God has given you to use for the Kingdom.

How has your childhood affected your perception of relationships or the way you view God?

How you view your father and other men can alter how you view God. Because God is our heavenly father, our minds will automatically shape the way we view God as the earthly father or male companion in our lives. If you don't have a relationship with your father, it may be hard for you to form a relationship with God. Here's the thing: God isn't a man, or should I say human. We can't view him as what we experience from people since His ways are not our ways, and His thoughts are not our thoughts. *(Isaiah 55:8-9 KJV)* Understand that God created you, and he knew you before you were formed in your mother's womb. *(Jeremiah 22:11)* He isn't absent. In fact, he is always with you. The Bible says that if you made your bed in hell, he is there; there is nowhere you can go that God can't find you. *(Psalms 139:7-12Psalms 139:7-10 KJV)* There is comfort, though to some, it could be taken as intimidation. However, know that God loves you, and you can't even imagine how deep His love is for you. *(Ephesians 3:18-19)* His patience with us is something none of us can even fathom. In fact, He decided that He needed to come down on earth to become a man (Jesus) so that He could free us from the bondage of sin and so we could get into heaven to be with Him. *(John 3:16)* God isn't petty or easily angered because of our shortcomings. He knows what we struggle with, and He knows how to help us overcome these obstacles. He knows who we need and who we don't. God is the answer, and when we put others in his place, that is where we begin to have issues.

Her Vision & Influences | 17

CURIOSITY

Virginity

Have you ever heard the phrase, "Curiosity killed the cat"? It's a common saying with a deeper truth. As we grow—whether in our faith or in life—we often observe what others are doing or get advice to try things that seem harmless. "What's the harm?" they say. But the Bible warns us about this. If we fall into the trap of "going with the flow" or experimenting out of curiosity, we risk making one mistake after another, which could ultimately alter the direction of our lives.

Back in high school, when I broke up with the long-term relationship I mentioned earlier, I formed this "trying to see something" mentality. Although I wanted to wait until marriage, I was really curious to find out if having sex with someone truly makes you fall in love and experience all those feelings. So, I started dating someone who was a pretty cool guy, but I didn't have any emotional attachments to him. After about three months of talking, I decided I wanted to lose my virginity and ended up giving myself away to him. I found myself in the backseat of my car, experiencing the worst pain I had ever felt at that point in my life, all for the sake of "trying to see something." Man, I know, pretty dumb, right? Here's the thing: often, when we find ourselves in a curious mindset, we end up making irrational decisions. Although when we're in the moment it makes all the sense in the world to satisfy that curious itch.

> *The Godly give good advice to their friends; the*
> *wicked lead them astray.*
>
> (Proverbs 12:26 NLT)

Drugs

I would always say that I am not one to be easily influenced. However, once I started dating, my mindset began to shift. After losing my virginity, I dated someone who was older and very attractive. At this point, I felt that in order to have a relationship with a guy and keep it, we had to have sex. I figured that I would get some practice in so I would be more experienced for the next guy I dated. Crazy, right? Eventually, another opportunity presented itself to "see something," and I was introduced to marijuana. I never had any interest in smoking, but the guy I dated always was. He kept asking me to try it, and eventually, I gave in and did. I remember the first time I smoked; it was the funniest scene ever. I was lying in bed with my boyfriend, and I took the blunt, inhaled it as hard as I could, and swallowed whatever I could get in my mouth. A few minutes later, I started feeling like I was floating in the air. But the downside was I couldn't lift my head. I was stuck lying down on the bed and could barely lift my arms. All I could do was laugh. As time passed, I continued smoking with him, but I didn't like the feeling when I smoked too much because I would start to feel nauseous. So, I learned how much I could handle to get "high enough." I never got hooked on it, but because he enjoyed the way I would become when I got high, I would do it for him on occasion. One day, God spoke to me, and He made me question why I was smoking in the first place. By this point, I had started changing myself to become the person my boyfriend wanted me to be. After about three years of dating, we got married, and making sure he was happy was my priority. The problem was: I wasn't happy. I had become someone I couldn't recognize, and I lost my personality. However, God helped me remember that I was naturally funny and full of life. I was using weed as the fix to my problem instead of turning to God, and this led to me becoming emotionally numb instead of the person I was meant to be.

> *"Bad company corrupts good character."*
>
> (1 Corinthians 15:33 NLT) }

When we allow people to influence us to do things we know are not right, the trend will continue and cause us to compromise our beliefs. We get to a point in our lives where we look up and, just like the float in the middle of the ocean, wonder how we got here. The company you keep can help steer you in the right direction or in the wrong one. The choice is yours to make.

COMPROMISE

When it comes to compromise, there are two paths we can take. One involves reaching a mutual agreement, where both sides work together to find a solution. The other involves being asked or pressured to do something that goes against your beliefs and your walk with Christ. Today, we're focusing on the second type— compromising in your faith. The challenge here is that it forces us to decide what or who matters most in the situation. In the end, this choice determines whether we will honor or dishonor God with our actions.

The other women

There was a time in my marriage when I grew tired, and I just wanted to prove to my husband that I could be the woman he desired. Instead, I found myself in a situation where his girlfriend, yes girlfriend, reached out, and she began coming on to me. She wanted to have a relationship with me, with or without him. I told him what she said, and he was excited about the idea. (Of course, he would be). She wanted me to be open-minded and just try it out with no pressure. I didn't want to because I knew that this wasn't right, and it ultimately went against my walk with Christ. In spite of this, He had already been so enticed about the idea that he told me it was going to happen. I remember taking a shower one day and thinking to myself, "Ok, I'm going to do this, and then I'm done with this marriage." I wanted to prove to him that I was "about that life", yep, another crazy decision. I went through with it, and I allowed her to do what she wanted to me. I had so many emotions going on in my head at that time. I was angry internally but I pretended like I was enjoying what was happening physically. I honestly just made a terrible mistake, and after it was all said and done, I felt disgusting. I was filled with so much shame and guilt because I knew that I had just sinned against God. I repented and asked God for forgiveness. Then I told my best friend what happened and faced the new issues I had just created for myself. So many things were wrong with this situation, but I want to focus on the fact that I willingly chose to dishonor God with my body. I chose to please my husband over pleasing God. Yes, we are called to submit to our spouses; however, we must first be submitted to God *(Ephesians 5:21-22)*, and when it comes to doing something that goes against God, we must choose to follow Christ over obeying our spouses or people, for that matter.

Am I now trying to win the approval of human beings or of God? Or am I trying to please people? If I were still trying to please people, I would not be a servant of Christ.

Galatians 1:10 NIV

Part Two

Hey girl, let's heal.

Chapter 4
HER CONFIDENCE
& BETRAYAL

etrayal is a sniper when it comes to losing confidence in yourself, your relationships, and your existence. Honestly, going through betrayal in the context of infidelity is one of the most painful experiences someone could go through outside of death itself. Whether you've been the one getting cheated on or you're the cheater, it's damaging on both ends of the spectrum. God never designed us to experience infidelity, adultery, fornication, or sexual sin. I know people like to argue about the men in the bible having multiple wives, amongst other sins, but I never saw anything saying that this was God's original design. The Bible mentions the expectations for marriage and the consequences when we choose to give in to sexual immorality. Let's address what God thinks about this real quick.

It's my body I can do what I want, right?

"You say, "I am allowed to do anything"—but not everything is good for you. And even though "I am allowed to do anything," I must not become a slave to anything. You say, "Food was made for the stomach, and the stomach for food." (This is true, though someday God will do away with both of them.) But you can't say that our bodies were made for sexual immorality. They were made for the Lord, and the Lord cares about our bodies. Don't you realize that your bodies are actually parts of Christ? Should a man take his body, which is part of Christ, and join it to a prostitute? Never! And don't you realize that if a man joins himself to a prostitute, he becomes one body with her? For the Scriptures say, "The two are united into one." But the person who is joined to the Lord is one spirit with him. Run from sexual sin! No other sin so clearly affects the body as this one does. For sexual immorality is a sin against your own body. Don't you realize that your body is the temple of the Holy Spirit, who lives in you and was given to you by God? You do not belong to yourself, for God bought you with a high price. So you must honor God with your body."

1 Corinthians 6:12–13, 15-20 NLT

This passage clearly states that when you give yourself to someone, you become "one" with them. Sex is the one thing that, if done outside of God's design, is actually sinning against your own body & you are destroying yourself *(Proverbs 6:32)*.

But I didn't have sex with them; it was just emotional...

> *But I say, anyone who even looks at a woman with lust has already committed adultery with her in his heart.*
>
> Matthew 5:28

Sex in marriage is God's design; anything outside of this will be judged by God Himself

> *"But because there is so much sexual immorality, each man should have his own wife, and each woman should have her own husband."*
>
> 1 Corinthians 7:2 NLT

> *"Give honor to marriage, and remain faithful to one another in marriage. God will surely judge people who are immoral and those who commit adultery."*
>
> Hebrews 13:4

God understands how painful it is to experience this because he has dealt with this, too. All throughout the Bible, we see Him compare Israel and Judah to being unfaithful to him. He called them prostitutes because every chance they got, they would go out and worship the same gods, or idols, that the other nations did. Even after all the blessings, mercy, and grace God continually gave, they continued to serve other deities. God's love for us is unexplainable, and because He knows that we are flawed, He sent His son to save us from the snares of sin. But this one sin, worshiping other gods, was and still remains a serious offense to God himself. This is why we, as believers in Jesus Christ, should be careful in what we choose to entertain for ourselves. Worldly things such as astrology, numerology, angel numbers, zodiac signs, horoscopes, palm readings, spirit guides, voodoo, love spells, chakras, yoga, yoni, etc. are not of God. All of these things are witchcraft, and when you practice them, you are serving other gods and idols (deities). If you are wondering if something you do is wrong or right, I encourage you to ask God. Read the book of *Jeremiah, Exodus 20:4, Leviticus 19:26, 19:31, and 20:6*; in the bible. I pray that you will receive an answer from God quickly concerning this in Jesus' Name.

The Betrayal

I first experienced betrayal at the age of 17 from the man I would later marry. I couldn't believe what my classmates would tell me. I remember someone told me her friend was talking to the same person I was with, and though it was hard for me to believe, I felt that there may have been some truth to it. Even though I dealt with infidelity while we were dating, I thought that marrying him would change everything and the cheating would stop. Once we actually got married, I figured that I had won the battle against those other women because I held the ultimate title: "Wifey."

What I didn't realize was that the war was just beginning. Infidelity didn't stop; he just got better at hiding it. I knew he wasn't faithful, but I couldn't prove it, so I turned into a private investigator and did things that I never thought I would just to catch my husband cheating. I had trackers, text forwarding, the whole nine! But no matter how much I found out, he would always deny it. I remember asking God to show me what I needed to see because I was tired of searching for proof and felt that my then husband wasn't being honest with me. Well, let's just say that once God answered that prayer, everything started to come out of the closet. Unfortunately, I wasn't ready for what God revealed to me, so I soon had to ask God to conceal anything else. My heart shattered as new information began to pour into my lap. I couldn't believe that all of this was happening to me. I fell into a deep depression, and I shut everyone out. I didn't want anything to do with God because I didn't understand why he allowed this to happen to me. I felt that my life was over, and I struggled to hold on to what I had left of my marriage. I grew so angry and bitter, and I wanted every one of those women to die. Yes, I know that's intense, but I'm just being honest about that season of my life. I didn't feel that I had anything to smile about. In fact, I grew emotionally numb, and because I cried so much, it got to the point where I was expecting the next thing to happen, and when it did, I had no tears left. The only emotion left to grow inside of me was anger. I turned away from God, but thankfully He did not turn away from me.

You may be experiencing or have experienced betrayal or infidelity in a relationship or marriage. So, I want to shine some light on how situations like this should be handled. Before you decide to get a divorce to try to work it out and to do all that you can to stay married. This could look like going to counseling together and/or individually as well as actively communicating with one another in an effort to work towards the process of healing your marriage. I have seen marriages that went through infidelity, and came out of the fire stronger. However, both the husband and wife have to be willing to put in the work to repair the damage that has been done. The one who committed infidelity has to be patient and understanding while their spouse goes through the healing stages from the damage they've caused. After all efforts have been exhausted, you are then free to get a divorce. The Bible explains that the reason people get divorced is because of our hardened hearts and unwillingness to forgive. I'd like to note that forgiveness doesn't always look like staying with the person you forgave. (We'll talk about this in another chapter) Know that God understands what you are going through, and because of this, He does not expect you to stay in a relationship with someone who has committed these acts against you. He knows how much it destroys you on the inside and could even destroy you physically on the outside. If you are unmarried and you are experiencing these things, I want to encourage you to take a look at yourself and ask, "Is it worth it?" because you are going through things that can be avoided. You are not married to this person, but yet you act as though you are. So, what does it benefit you to continue to be in a relationship with someone who has proven to be unfaithful to you prior to getting married? This should be a clear sign to you to let this relationship go, especially if the behavior is repetitive. Take some time to be single and really give God the opportunity to heal your heart, mend your broken pieces, and show you what love really is.

Comparison

I didn't understand why he couldn't be faithful to me, so I began to ask him about the other women. It was clear that looks really didn't play a part in the matter. It was more about the way they made him feel. These women would do anything for him; they made him feel alive and like he was the best thing walking on two legs. He received satisfaction from showing them who I was and hearing that they would be willing to be with me, too, so that they could continue to be with him. He would also tell me personal information about his other women like, "this girl only wore Victoria's Secret" and he would explain how into him she was. He would describe them in such an attractive way so when I finally saw them for myself, I was shocked because I felt like they were no comparison to me. But it's true what they say... "It's not all about the looks." Some women are so desperate that they are willing to do anything to keep a man that doesn't even belong to them. Because those women found a man who loved the attention and it stroked his ego, it appeared that he was winning. Despite their appearance, I compared myself to them and I too, began to exclusively wear Victoria's Secret. I amped up my sex game and tried to be everything he desired me to be. I remember after an intimate moment I asked him if he enjoyed it, and he assured me that he did and I should know because of how he reacted in the moment. Then I asked if he was satisfied; why couldn't he stay faithful to me? His response was that he didn't know. It was at that moment I realized that no matter how much I did, he still wouldn't be faithful to me. It wasn't about the people he couldn't leave alone; this was an internal issue that had nothing to do with me. Comparing myself to other women took away my confidence and increased my insecurities. I thought something was wrong with me, and it tore me to pieces.

Truth is, I didn't know who I was because if I had, I wouldn't have allowed myself to stay in that situation for as long as I did. Comparing yourself is like telling God that He made a mistake when He created you. God knew you before you were formed

Comparing yourself is like telling God that He made a mistake when He created you

in your mother's womb. He created you just the way you are for a purpose. When you desire to be like others, you move further away from who God created you to be. You start to look at yourself with dissatisfaction and think that everyone else is better than you are. You get in lanes you were never supposed to be in. You do things outside of your character. You may even wish you could just be someone else so you can have what you see in them. You will get to the point where you dislike the person you compare yourself to just because you can never be them. Why do we put ourselves in such an ugly mindset? If they can't see and appreciate who you are, you don't need them in your life. Never allow anyone to turn you against yourself. You may not be perfect, but you are worth it, and don't forget Jesus thought you were worth dying for.

Chapter 5

HER BREAKDOWN (BROKEN & TIRED)

*Letting go isn't quitting; it's recognizing
you are not the one in control.*

Sometimes, we want something so badly that we overlook the facts and signs telling us it's not worth pursuing. We somehow think that things will change and we will have our happy ending. But the whole time, God has been trying to show us that this isn't his plan for our lives. Are you willing to let go of what you think is good for you for the best that God already has for you?

Accepting the facts

You can't force or manufacture true change in anyone, regardless of how badly you want it. You can compromise, beg and plead, stick it out, pray, and fast, but the truth is, as people, we have to want it for ourselves. Only through God can one truly change. During my journey of holding on to my marriage for dear life, I realized that I didn't have any control over what he did (no matter how noisy I became). In fact, it's being in denial that can be the most damaging to our minds. Rejecting the truth and pretending that nothing is going on is like slowly killing yourself from the inside out. You'll begin convincing yourself that maybe they're telling the truth when in reality, the story is far from it. You'll think that you are the one who is crazy, and honestly, you are. Yep, I said it! What's crazy is that you can sit there

> *Only through God can one truly change*

and purposely believe a lie while pretending nothing has happened for the sake of keeping peace and the relationship. It's a hard truth, but I don't believe that this strategy is effective at all. When we get out of denial and accept the truth that is presented to us, we can begin to make decisions that will best benefit our lives. There's a difference between having faith and closing your eyes to what you don't want to believe. In *John 5:1-15,* Jesus asked the lame man one question, "Do you want to be healed?" The man said yes, and Jesus said take up your mat and walk. Notice that the man had a choice in if he wanted to be healed or not. Well, looking at this from a different perspective, if the person you are believing will change one day doesn't want that change for themselves, then it won't happen. God knows what it takes for each of us, and sometimes, we have to understand what our positions are in that person's life. One plants the seeds, and God will send someone else to water. I know this may not be something most want to hear, but I believe if it were meant for you to stay in a relationship that is toxic, God would have given you the grace to do so. We have to reach a point where we give that person to God. You can try praying this: "God, I take my hands off, I can't change them because I am not you. Only you can reach them the way they need it. Only you can turn this situation around; only you can save them. God, I release them to you, and I remove my expectations of them to be who I want them to be. God heal their heart, fill every void, and wiped every tear they didn't shed. Open their eyes, Lord, so they can see and ears so they can hear. God, they need you, and I need you."

The best thing you can do is trust God to do what only he can do. Release all bitterness, unforgiveness, and the grasp you have on them. You are only hurting yourself the longer you hold on.

Letting Go

Once you reach the point where you no longer want to fight or cry, you no longer want to force, beg, and plead. You start to look at things for what they are. You now realize that letting go is necessary in order to step in the direction that God is leading you. Here's the thing: if we are not careful, people can become idols in our lives and cause us to not only disobey God but to desire them more than we desire God. When you want them so badly, you are willing to do anything to keep them or make them happy and that is nothing but a trap that leads you further away from God.

During the process of separation before divorce, I still questioned my decision. I still had a strong desire for change. I wanted him to show me how serious he was about our marriage, that he didn't want the other women anymore, and that he was ready to do what it would take to work on our marriage. But even through that, God revealed to me that he was still holding on to someone else. He still had the "just in case we don't work out woman" around. I waited to see a glimmer of hope, but it never came. Anytime I thought about staying, memories of all the pain I was going through flashed through my mind as a reminder of why I was making this decision. I still prayed and asked God for guidance, but everything pointed me to go through with it. I know people may disagree and say God would never tell you to divorce your spouse. But the thing is, they aren't God, so how would they know? As I've pointed out in the previous chapter, biblically, there are cases when divorce is acceptable to God. I believe that God cares more about your mental and physical well-being than staying in something that is ultimately killing you. Ask yourself if you have done all that you could do to save your marriage. Have you gone to counseling? Have you evaluated yourself in the situation and given

God room to show you yourself? If so, and you know in your heart that this is the end, you have to let it go. It wasn't until I let go that I could really begin to heal.

Chapter 6

HER HEALING & FORGIVENESS

Forgiveness is needed to truly heal.

Healing and forgiveness go hand in hand. In order to heal, you have to be willing to forgive. I know it may be hard, but holding on to unforgiveness is more damaging to yourself than it is to them.

The Healing Process

At the beginning of my healing journey, I dove head first into getting my relationship right with God. However, I couldn't fully heal because I was still attached to what was hurting me. Healing can become difficult when you are still in the same environment or with the same people. It's like becoming injured, and instead of protecting and caring for your wound, more pain is inflicted, causing it to become worse. In the same way, you can't expect to heal if you are still attached to the person who is causing you pain. People and environments can hold you back, but it is up to us to make the decision to separate ourselves and heal. Remember you aren't healing for just yourself, you're healing for someone else too. It's time to reconnect with yourself and become the woman God created you to be.

> *You can't expect to heal if you are still attached to the person who is causing you pain*

The Need for Community

After my divorce, I was introduced to a community called "TOU" (The One University). I took their courses on becoming one with God, healing, and working out the deeper issues I was dealing with. It was like God was smiling at me, saying, "I got you." I mean, it was everything I needed in that season; I met some great people and felt that God was equipping me with the necessary tools to continue my journey of becoming whole.

I remember God led me to Transformation Church in Tulsa, Oklahoma, and I would watch their services online often. During that time, I needed to have the word taught, not preached. I started to understand the word in a new, more practical way. It was like learning to ride a bike and really focusing on truly learning about God. I had known of God before, but it was up to me to know him for myself. From there, I was challenged to go to church physically, and ironically, after I asked God if this was necessary, that next Sunday, Tim Ross spoke at Transformation church and said, "You need to get in a church physically." I was shocked because it was very direct, and I knew that God was answering me. So I asked God where He wanted me to go because I didn't want to just go anywhere. Soon after that experience, Michael Todd came to speak in Dallas, TX, at Embassy City, and I almost didn't go, but I decided to attend. I had never heard of this church. As a matter of fact, I thought I was going to the Embassy Suites (the known hotel chain). When I got there and saw Tim Ross, I remember thinking, "Oh, that's nice he is here to support Michael," not realizing that this was his church! Once I connected the dots, I knew that this was the church God wanted me to join. I grew more spiritually and went from knowing God for myself to developing a deeper relationship with Him.

I learned that healing and growth aren't independent journeys; you still need people. Although you need to develop a personal relationship with God, being a part of a community with other believers will encourage, inspire, and empower you as you grow. The Bible talks about iron sharpening iron *(Proverbs 27:17)*, so it is imperative to surround yourself with people who are walking down the same path you are. You need support as well as people who will pray and fast with and for you. You need people who will steer you in the right direction when things get challenging. You need to see an example of what it looks like to walk with God.

> *"As iron sharpens iron, so a friend sharpens a friend."*
>
> Proverbs 27:17 NLT

Are you really healed?

I was faced with this question after a dream one day. I personally felt that I was completely healed since I held no bitterness in my heart towards my ex-husband. I had forgiven him, and I was good, or that's what I thought to myself. But God has a funny way of showing us the hidden areas in our lives so we can continue to advance and not become hindered in our growth. This was my dream:

My best friend and I went out to a big place which I called a theater. Many people were there, including people I recognized. On the way in, there were jaguars simply lying around, unbothered by their surroundings. Some were black, and some were spotted. We decided to leave the theater and walk into a long strip of connected stores. It was like a long hall with doors separating them. I had on a long black fur coat that seemed to be made from an animal, possibly the jaguar, and my friend had on the spotted fur coat. We began walking through the halls, and two of the jaguars began following us. My friend walked in a different direction, and both cats began following me, making a low panting noise. I was uncomfortable with the idea of being followed, so I kept walking to get away from them and blocked one of them as I closed a door. The black one, however, still followed and lightly rubbed its paw against my leg. I could also see its nails as it rubbed against me, but it didn't scratch me. I tried to close a door to trap it, but the door kept opening. The people on the other side were against it, and one girl seemed to be afraid of the jaguar. So I walked through the store to reach the outside door, hoping to trap the cat outside. But when I opened the door and tried to get the cat out, I woke up.

I also had another dream about my ex-husband and I being at peace with one another with no drama or a romantic connection, just friend-like interactions.

God is the one who gives insight into what dreams truly mean

I spoke with a Holy Spirit-led dream interpreter (this is important because God is the one who gives insight into what dreams truly mean), and he told me that there was something that I valued greatly in life that was also causing me a lot of pain. This ultimately felt like a heavy and consistent burden at the time, and when I attempted to separate myself from it, I was not successful.

I sat with this for a while and asked God what the heavy burden was. I thought maybe it was the passing of my mother, but that did not speak to me. Then I thought about my ex-husband, and I began to feel heavy. At that point, I knew that he was a part of this, but I wasn't sure why. I journaled and began to talk to God about this, asking for his guidance and clarity. God began to show me that I hadn't let go of the pain my ex-husband caused so that I could truly move forward. I had let go of the offense that led to our failed marriage but, I didn't realize that I was still suffering because of what took place after the divorce. I listed out everything that could have possibly been the cause of my pain, and this is what God revealed to me:

1. *I needed to forgive myself for the betrayal I inflicted on me.* I knew that I shouldn't have stayed as long as I did. I ignored that voice inside and the warnings telling me to let it go, and I forced myself to stay. I knew I shouldn't have gotten married, but I did it anyway. I kept secrets from my parents when all they wanted to do was help me. I had to forgive myself for the pain I put myself through.

2. *I needed to let go of my expectations.* I badly wanted to have a cordial relationship with my ex-husband, even a friendship. So that we could be at peace with one another and co-parent in a healthy manner. I also wanted him to apologize for what he did to me. I wanted him to be present for the kids and to be the father that they needed. I wanted him to be the man I knew he could be.

Holding on to these things caused me to put my hope in my expectations instead of in God. Hope deferred makes the heart sick *(Proverbs 13:12)*. I couldn't understand why he wouldn't

> When we put our hope in God, we are saying to God, I trust you with this, and I know that you will take care of it. I know that all things will work out for my good according to your purposes for my life (Romans 8:28)

change, why he kept up all the things he did, why he wouldn't be honest, and why he wouldn't own up to the pain he inflicted on me and in our relationship. I couldn't understand how he could completely turn into someone that I didn't recognize. I didn't understand how he could hate me so much when I walked away for the purpose of him living the life he couldn't let go of. I couldn't understand how he chose not to be a father. I was left with a series of thoughts, and none of them were going to help me truly heal. At this point, I realized that I needed to put my hope in God alone. The Bible tells us not to put our hope in a man *(Psalms 146:3)*. When we put our hope in God, we are saying to God, I trust you with this, and I know that you will take care of it. I know that all things will work out for my good according to your purposes for my life *(Romans 8:28)*. When we place our expectations on people, we will be disappointed when they don't amount to them. We can't control what people will do or how they will respond to situations. We must decide to let them go and walk in the freedom that only God can give.

Forgiveness

Understand that forgiveness is more for you than it is for the person you seek it from. Holding on to unforgiveness is like drinking poison and waiting for someone else to die from it. Forgiving them doesn't mean that they did nothing wrong or that you're excusing what happened. It's freeing you from the cell of unforgiveness. If you choose to hold on to unforgiveness, it will cause bitterness, resentment, anger, pride, oppression, and more inside you.

I had to choose to forgive him for what he did to me so that I could heal instead of being bitter and angry. Don't wait for people to apologize because that may never happen. When you forgive, you should set boundaries and decide if you will allow that person to have access to you.

> *"If you forgive those who sin against you, your heavenly Father will forgive you. But if you refuse to forgive others, your Father will not forgive your sins."*
>
> Matthew 6:14–15

Forgiveness is a process, and depending on the offense, it may require you to forgive more than once. When dealing with an issue like betrayal or an experience that broke you, time is needed to genuinely forgive and heal. It starts with saying, "I forgive you for..." or "God, I forgive them for..." and by faith, you have forgiven them. But what if it doesn't feel like you forgave them? What if you're still bothered by what happened, and when you see them or hear their name, your emotions rise? You have to know that those feelings are normal, and the process of full forgiveness has only begun. The Bible talks about forgiving someone over and over again in *(Matthew 18:22)*. This doesn't mean that we forgive the person for the same offense and continue to allow them to do the same thing repeatedly. It means that you will need to go through the process of forgiving them for what they did until it no longer hurts. Eventually, you will reach a state of forgiveness. The memory of the event will be there, but the emotional damage and pain will be gone, and you will be able to move past what happened.

How do you know you've healed by forgiving someone?

A: "When it no longer bothers you and you can move past what happened."

Don't look back

What you choose to focus on is where you'll eventually end up. Once you've decided to walk down the path of healing, you have to stand by your decision to reach the version you were always meant to become. It's easy to start reminiscing on the past, the good moments you shared with them, how they made you feel, or you may even get to a point where you become afraid and feel that you've made a mistake and can't do life without them. It's normal, and it's a process that most of us go through. Each time I began to get into this mindset, God instantly reminded me why I made the decision in the first place. It's not going to be easy. But because you know that remaining in the same situation will not only bring harm to you, it will also stop you from being who you were called to be. You have to let them go and focus on your future so you can break the cycle and begin a new path that only God can lead you down. This new version of yourself is healed, whole, and walking in your purpose.

Part Three

Hey girl, let's thrive.

Chapter 7

HER PURPOSE & CALLING

You were created to do great works.

Y ou have a specific purpose and call that is unique to who God created you to be. *Jeremiah 33:11* says that He knew you before you were formed in your mother's womb, and his plans are to prosper you, not to harm you. This means that God was intentional when he created you and felt that you were needed on earth. God has given everyone spiritual gifts to use for the Kingdom, and you also have unique talents and skills that come naturally to you. However, every believer's ultimate purpose is to bring glory to God in everything they do.

> *God was intentional when he created you and felt that you were needed on earth*

How to identify what your purpose is

Ask yourself in what area you feel the most attacked or insecure. If we pay attention to the different things that are happening in our lives, we can better identify how to partner with God. It is often the very thing you don't want to do. From a young age, speaking and being in the spotlight was always a fear of mine. I can recall the horror of standing on stage as a young child dressed for an Easter program and my mom bending over trying to get me to speak in front of the congregation. As I became older, God would be the one training me to speak, and I struggled terribly. I started working with kids as a junior in high school, and one of my responsibilities was to manage them effectively. There would be anywhere between 50-100 kids at a time, and the only way to get their attention was through a firm directive. Every time I knew I had to exercise my voice to be heard, my heart would beat through my chest, and my hands were two pools of sweat. However, once my mouth opened, I would relax. From there, I began leading groups of 6-8 adults, and eventually, that number grew to more than 20 at a time! There was even a time when I was invited to speak at a leaders meeting for a school district I managed. The room was full of all the leaders in the district, including principals, superintendents, board members, administrators, etc. I was very nervous, but I got it done because it was my job. I stood tall in front of those leaders and said exactly what I needed to say, smiled, and went home. Even though I was filled with nerves, I not only overcame my fear, I also received a call saying that I did an amazing job. God was setting me up for something greater and this time it would be for the Kingdom. I used to have feelings that led me to believe my voice had no value, and I struggled with being belittled to the point where I thought that I didn't make sense when I spoke. But I've grown to realize that it was all an attempt to silence my voice for good. However, the enemy had no idea that I would find my voice and allow God to lead the way. Now, I have been able to speak at events virtually and in person about God and business, and it has been a journey I am grateful to have experienced.

Your purpose is tied to what God calls you to do, and it may not look the same in every season. For example, When I worked for the school district, my purpose was to run excellent programs

Your purpose is tied to what God calls you to do, and it may not look the same in every season

and provide a safe space for children, parents, and schools while pouring into the youth. Once that season ended, my purpose shifted to something different. One mistake many people make is getting purpose and identity confused. You can work or be a part of something for years, and when it's over, you feel like a part of you just died. That's because you found your identity in what it was you were doing instead of the purpose of why you were there. Think of it this way: we are on an assignment, and when God calls you, it is your turn to use the gifts, skills, lessons, and talents within you to do what He has assigned you to do. This doesn't mean the assignment is permanent because once you complete the task, God has another one to come. *What* He created you to do may not change, but *where* He wants you to do it can.

Spiritual Gifts

1 Corinthians 12

Word of wisdom, word of knowledge, faith, healing, working of miracles, prophecy, discerning of spirits, divers kinds of tongues, interpretation of tongues, teacher, serving, encourager, giving, leading, kindness

1 Peter 4:10 - 11

God has given each of you a gift from his great variety of spiritual gifts. Use them well to serve one another. Do you have the gift of speaking? Then speak as though God himself were speaking through you. Do you have the gift of helping others? Do it with all the strength and energy that God supplies. Then, everything you do will bring glory to God through Jesus Christ. All glory and power to him forever and ever! Amen.

What are you naturally good at?

You have unique skills crafted inside of you, and they have developed over time. Think about what you can do easily. What do people always come to you for? Ask your parents or people close to you what they think you're good at. Doing this will help you identify things that you're naturally gifted at if you are unaware. When I was younger, I found myself taking an interest in computers. My mother was a computer programmer, and my dad would build computers, so naturally, I was good at working and understanding technology. As I began to work and help others in that field, I started to notice other areas I was good in and found myself leading and instructing people on how to do certain things. I realized that being a leader and teaching was a spiritual gift that God had given me. As I grew spiritually, I began understanding that these are gifts that I could use for the Kingdom, and they are all things that circle around what I have been called to do.

Your Calling

Your calling is where God is leading you. Your purpose is what God is calling you to do once you get there. We often use the terms "purpose" and "calling" interchangeably; however, they are very different. When you are "called," you have the responsibility to answer the call.

> *Your calling is where God is leading you. Your purpose is what God is calling you to do once you get there*

Let's look at Moses' story in the Bible. Moses was a natural leader, saved for a greater purpose. One day, he decided to take action and defend one of his people from the Egyptians. Although he was raised by the Egyptian princess, he didn't experience the hardships his people faced. Still, he recognized their unfair treatment. In a moment of passion, Moses killed an Egyptian to protect one of his own, then fled in fear for his life. Moses was born to lead, a gift given by God. While going about his daily life, God called him to deliver His people from Egyptian oppression. Moses now had the chance to fulfill his calling and use his God-given gift of leadership. Though hesitant at first, as we often are when called to step outside our comfort zones, Moses eventually answered. With God by his side, he carried out his mission. You don't need to search for your calling—God will guide you to it. To learn more about Moses's story, you can read Exodus in the bible.

Chapter 8

DISCERNING GOD'S VOICE

Is that you God?

G od speaks to us in different ways, but our ability to hear or understand Him can be affected by our relationship with Him and how well we know His character...

Impressions

When I was a kid, I used to get feelings or prompts to do things that I did not want to do. They weren't bad things; they just made me feel uncomfortable. Anytime this would happen, I would feel a resistance, as if something was tugging at me. But I resisted because it was something that I was afraid to do. For example, I may have felt a nudge to say something to somebody, but because of the fear of what I thought may happen, I didn't want to do it, and I would ignore those feelings. I didn't realize that God was the one speaking to me until I became an adult and grew closer in my relationship with Him.

I was leaving the store one day when I approached a guy standing outside selling CDs. I didn't have any money to support him, so I walked past him and headed straight to the car. Once I got in, I began feeling an impression, prompting me to write a note and give it to him. At the time, I thought this was a silly idea because I knew that this man clearly wanted money. So, I decided to dismiss the thought and go on with my day. As I left the parking lot, God reminded me of what I said to Him before. I told God that I was going to listen to him the next time I felt these nudges, and here I was leaving the parking lot. As I was driving away, I felt convicted and decided to turn around. I wrote the note, drove up, and gave it to him. I told him, "I don't have any cash, but I want to give you this note and encourage you to keep going." After that, I drove off and went about my business.

I'm not sure what impact it had on the man, but often, we don't see why God asks us to do certain things. It's when we step aside and trust Him that His perfect plan unfolds. Sometimes, God lets us see the reason behind it, and it always has a purpose. I encourage you to take action when you feel prompted by God. Be obedient and follow through. It may feel intimidating because we never know what God will ask of us, but I promise you, it's always worth it, and it's an honor to be part of His plan.

Dreams

God is always speaking to us, but when we're awake, we often rely on rational thinking. We might see signs or hear something that suggests God is speaking, but we dismiss it because we're focused on logic. However, when we're asleep, our logical minds are at rest, allowing God more freedom to communicate what He wants to tell us..

I remember asking God repeatedly if the guy I was talking to was meant to be my husband. Let's dive into that for a moment. I really liked him, but I never felt 100% sure he was the one. I prayed constantly, saw signs, but still needed a more direct answer. I didn't want to make the wrong choice and go through another divorce.

God answered in many ways, but the clearest response came through a dream. In the dream, there was a girl who, for some reason, didn't like me. I asked if we could talk, and we went into another room. She told me, "If you make the decision now, you will start a new season. There's something that looks like God but isn't. If you act now instead of waiting, you'll make the wrong decision and cause a delay." As she spoke, I thought about marrying the guy, and I began to cry. When I turned back to look for her, she was gone. When I woke up, I realized it was a clear message and a warning I needed to pay attention to.

If you are a dreamer or have frequent dreams, I encourage you to write them down or record yourself describing them as soon as you wake up. God may be trying to send you a message. Here are a few signs that your dream might be from God: you keep having the same type of dream repeatedly, certain parts of the dream stick with you, or the dream feels unsettling or scary.

I've learned that sometimes God uses dreams to give insight into something that's coming, something you've been praying about, or even as a warning to help you prepare. If you're unsure whether a dream is good or bad, always pray and ask God for clarity. Speak against anything the enemy might be trying to do, and ask for God's protection and for His will to be done. To learn more about dreams I encourage you to read about Joseph (Jesus' earthly father) in Matthew 1: 20 -21, 2:13, 2:19 -20, 2:22, Joseph in Genesis 37, 39, 40-50, and Daniel in the book of Daniel in the bible.

People & Things

God speaks to us through people and the world around us. Sometimes, He addresses things we haven't even prayed about. You might be in the middle of a conversation, and something is said that speaks directly to your situation.

I remember going through a tough time, and all I could do was cry the entire day. I prayed to God for help, and when I opened my Bible, I came across two scriptures that spoke directly to me.

One of the passages of scripture was Isaiah 40:27-31:

> *O Jacob, how can you say the Lord does not see your troubles? O Israel, how can you say God ignores your rights? Have you never heard? Have you never understood?*
>
> *The Lord is the everlasting God, the Creator of all the earth. He never grows weak or weary. No one can measure the depths of his understanding. He gives power to the weak and strength to the powerless. Even youths will become weak and tired, and young men will fall in exhaustion. But those who trust in the Lord will find new strength. They will soar high on wings like eagles. They will run and not grow weary. They will walk and not faint.*

After crying out to God and asking for the strength He promised in scripture, I decided to go hiking to clear my mind. While on the trail, I came across a family, and the little girl asked her father, "But what if it doesn't happen?" The father replied, "It's going to happen." Hearing this, I was taken aback, as it felt oddly relevant to my own situation, but I kept moving. As I walked past them, the father then asked the little girl, "Are you okay, Princess?" That moment hit me hard—it felt like he was speaking directly to me. Tears started streaming down my face, and I began to jog to distance myself from them. In that instant, I knew God was speaking to me through that man, even though he had no idea. Strangely enough, I sat down further along the trail, and though many people I had passed before walked by, I never saw that family again.

> "But what if it doesn't happen?" The father replied, "It's going to happen."

That day, I experienced God as a Comforter. He let me know that He sees me, He cares for me, and that He understands my pain. He assured me that "it was going to happen."

Here's another moment when God spoke to me after I asked for a sign. I remember a girl reaching out to me on Facebook, telling me she was in need. She explained that she was living in her car, her phone was about to die, and she needed money to get by. Something about her story felt off, so I prayed and asked God for a sign to know if I should help her or if she was being dishonest.

At that time in my life, I had just started speaking publicly about God online and wasn't used to people reaching out like this. That same night, I had a terrible toothache and got up at midnight to go to the store for something to ease the pain. On my way home, I noticed an old car in front of me with a license plate that said something like "not real" or "fake." I don't remember the exact wording, but it was clear. When I saw that license plate, I knew it was the sign God sent to answer my prayer.

God is intentional, and when you ask Him to speak to you, He will—you just need to listen. If you're struggling to hear Him, pray for God to open your eyes and ears so you can see and hear what He is doing.

Audibly

I haven't personally experienced hearing an audible voice from God, but I won't limit how He chooses to speak to others. When people say they've heard an audible voice, I don't doubt them because it's not my place to judge. It just hasn't been my experience. The closest I've come to hearing God audibly was when a man called my name on a hiking trail.

I encourage you to spend some time in God's presence by reading His word and talking to Him. As you grow deeper in your relationship with God, everything will begin to change. You will begin to understand God's character and His desires for your life. The Bible tells us to meditate on His word day and night. So the more you do this, the more you will hear and understand what God is saying to you. When God speaks to you, it will not contradict His word - if it does, it's not God. This is why it's so important to read your Bible for yourself.

Chapter 9

THINGS THAT BLOCK GOD'S VOICE

God is speaking..are you listening?

Be open to hearing, listening, and obeying.

We must be open to hearing and accepting what God has to say. Sometimes, we may doubt that God will speak to us, and when the Holy Spirit does, we end up disobeying or ignoring Him. If we continue to ignore the Holy Spirit, we will eventually stop hearing God's voice. This is crucial to understand because, like any relationship, if you keep ignoring someone, communication will eventually cease. If God is calling you to do something or stop something, it's your responsibility to listen and obey.

Environment

Your environment can block God's voice as well. The people you hang around, your surroundings, and things that you choose to do can block God's voice. God is not limited to reaching us, but when you are constantly in environments that are contradictory to the way you should live and you're around people who have no interest in

> *Sometimes, you have to separate yourself from people who don't add to your life or those who pull you away from God*

growing their relationship with God, these things can affect the way you think. When you believe God isn't speaking to you, it may be because you are too consumed with the things of this world. Sometimes, you have to separate yourself from people who don't add to your life or those who pull you away from God because they're influencing you to continue being the same person that you used to be. These are not people you need to have a close relationship with when you are growing in your relationship with God.

Surround yourself with people who are growing in their relationship with God or have already reached a level in their walk with Christ that you aspire to. As I mentioned in the community section of the previous chapter, your community is important. You can read the Word all day, but if you keep returning to the same environments, you can't expect true change or to hear God clearly. When you start truly growing in your relationship with God, you'll begin to feel uncomfortable or convicted when trying to do the things you used to because your desires will start to change.

Every day, we either feed our spirit with the Word of God or the things of the world. Just like with food, you can choose to consume what's healthy or what's harmful, but either way, you're feeding yourself daily. The same applies to your spirit—you need to be mindful of what you consume, whether it's what you watch, listen to, or participate in, because it influences your spiritual well-being.

For example, if you're trying to stay abstinent but constantly expose yourself to music or shows that focus on sex, don't be surprised if you find yourself in a compromising situation, giving in to temptation. What you take in will eventually show up in your actions.

When you're committed to living a changed life, you begin to shift what you entertain and feed your spirit. Pay attention to the Holy Spirit when you feel that inner nudge to avoid certain things—don't ignore it. The Holy Spirit is there to help you, but it's up to you to make the choice to follow that guidance.

Silence the noise

Sometimes, we need to block out unnecessary voices. Ask God to silence any voice that sounds like His but isn't so you can hear Him clearly. This may also mean stepping away from distractions you've been entertaining. You might need to take a break from social media, stop watching TV, or limit how many pastors and sermons you listen to. Constantly jumping from one sermon to another can confuse you about what God is really saying because you're listening to too many perspectives when He may want you to focus on just one. Pray and ask God who you should be listening to in this season, then focus on that person.

> *Ask God to silence any voice that sounds like His but isn't so you can hear Him clearly*

Consider fasting to reconnect with God and hear His voice more clearly. Whether it's for a few hours or days, let yourself be led by what feels right for you. If you have any health issues, check with your doctor first. During your fast, take time to pray, read His word, and write down anything you notice or hear. God will meet you where you are; all you need to do is take the first step and give Him space to respond.

Chapter 10

THE HOLD OF FEAR

Be strong and courageous; God is with you.

If you are not careful, fear can paralyze you from moving forward, and it will cause you to remain stagnant instead of making progress toward who you are called to be. It is our job to speak against the fears and the thoughts that we have in our heads so that we can actually walk into God's calling over our lives.

When deciding whether to get a divorce, one of my biggest fears was worrying about what others would think. We often care too much about how people perceive us, fearing that we'll disappoint them or be seen as failures. But I had to come to terms with the fact that this is my life. Why should I let someone else's opinion stop me from making an important decision for my own well-being?

It is our job to speak against the fears and the thoughts that we have in our heads

The next fear I had to overcome was sharing my testimony when God said it was time. I had to confront the reality that some people might not like what I had to say because it would affect them. But I realized that if God has set me free and wants me to use my voice to help someone else avoid the same mistakes I made, who am I to withhold that? God revealed to me that my disobedience could delay someone else's freedom. God didn't deliver me from my situation just for my sake. He gave me a testimony to share with others and offer them hope. The Bible says that we overcome by the blood of the Lamb and by our testimony. *(Revelation 12:11)* We are called to share what God has done in our lives, not to keep silent. Our testimonies are something the enemy cannot take from us. No one can deny what you've experienced with God because it's your story, and the world needs to hear it. God will guide you on who to share your testimony with. Not everyone is called to share their story on a large platform, but God will place people in your life who need to hear how you made it through so they can, too.

You need to reach a point where you don't care who hears what you have to say—speak because God has called you to do so. If you let others control you, you'll never fully walk in the purpose God has for you. After you've gone through healing, you must overcome the fear of retaliation, criticism, or others' opinions. We are called to rise above that. We are called to stand up for what's right, to speak up when others stay silent, and to proclaim the truth.

That said, I'm not suggesting you share every detail of your life or things that don't serve a purpose. When it comes to sharing your testimony or story, it should be meaningful and helpful to those you're speaking to. Ask yourself: Why are you sharing this? Is it to stir up drama, to expose someone, or are you sincerely trying to help someone? Not every part of your story needs to be told to everyone who will listen. God will guide you to specific people, where sharing the more personal details will have a greater impact. These individuals may need to hear your experience because God is doing something specific in their lives. Pray for wisdom to know when, what, and with whom to share your story.

Once you overcome fear and stop worrying about what others think, nothing will be able to stop you. Paul reminds us, "Am I now trying to win the approval of human beings, or of God? If I were still trying to please people, I would not be a servant of Christ." *(Galatians 1:10)*. You can't focus on others because they are not your God. Your priority should be what God thinks and being obedient to Him.

I also advise against sharing certain parts of your story publicly until you've taken the time to heal. It's difficult to speak about something while you're still going through it. Your testimony should come from a place of healing, where you're living in that truth. Remember, our words should uplift and encourage others, showing them that if God did it for you, He can do it for them, too. That's the power of a testimony—it not only inspires others but also reminds you that if God did it once, He can do it again. It strengthens your faith and gives you encouragement. So, don't be afraid to share, but use wisdom in how you share it, ensuring it's always edifying.

> *"Am I now trying to win the approval of human beings, or of God? If I were still trying to please people, I would not be a servant of Christ."* (Galatians 1:10)

Chapter 11

OVERCOME
MENTAL BATTLES

Get out of your head & get on the battlefield.

You have the power to fight the mental battles in your mind. The Bible tells us to take our thoughts captive and to put on the full armor of God (2 Corinthians 10:5 & Ephesians 6:10-18). If you hear voices in your head saying things like "You can't do it," "You're not smart enough," "You've made too many mistakes," or "No one will ever love you,"—remember that they're not true because they're not of God. Whenever negative thoughts are planted, I want you to understand that you must fight them by speaking truth over yourself. This might sound unusual, but it's essential. Combat negative thoughts with the Word of God. For every negative thought, find a scripture that counters it and declare it over your life. If you think you're worthless or unlovable, say: "I am fearfully and wonderfully made. I thank God for making me so beautifully complex. I am God's masterpiece. I am more than a conqueror through Christ Jesus." This will silence the negative voices. If you don't respond, the thoughts will continue. So as soon as a negative thought arises, counter it with the Word of God.

> "A final word: Be strong in the Lord and in his
> mighty power. Put on all of God's armor so that
> you will be able to stand firm against all strategies
> of the devil. For we are not fighting against flesh-
> and-blood enemies, but against evil rulers and
> authorities of the unseen world, against mighty
> powers in this dark world, and against evil spirits
> in the heavenly places. Therefore, put on every
> piece of God's armor so you will be able to resist the
> enemy in the time of evil. Then after the battle you
> will still be standing firm. Stand your ground,
> putting on the belt of truth and the body armor of
> God's righteousness. For shoes, put on the peace that
> comes from the Good News so that you will be fully
> prepared. In addition to all of these, hold up the
> shield of faith to stop the fiery arrows of the devil.
> Put on salvation as your helmet, and take the sword
> of the Spirit, which is the word of God."

Ephesians 6:10–17 NLT

I encourage you to write down all the negative things you tell yourself or what the enemy is telling you. Then, I want you to find a scripture that speaks the opposite of that negative thought and write it down. You can make some flashcards, put them in your phone, or whatever is feasible. Just be sure to have it handy, so the next time you feel attacked, you can go to war with the truth.

When you find yourself dealing with negative emotions, such as depression, anger, sadness, etc., I want you to ask yourself two questions: "Why do I feel like this?" and "What happened to make me feel this way." After answering the questions, take time to pray. If you're unsure what triggered your emotions, ask God to reveal the cause. Often, small things can build up over time and create bigger emotional reactions. For example, I have a seven-year-old who can be very strong-willed. Sometimes, she has meltdowns and gives me a hard time, which takes an emotional toll on me. If I let those feelings consume my mind, the next small inconvenience will feel much bigger, and I'll become overwhelmed with emotions. Soon, everything piles up, and before I know it, my whole day feels ruined. I'm left feeling sad, frustrated, and in a negative mood. But it's important not to let that happen. As soon as a negative thought enters your mind, you must make the choice not to agree with it and let it take over.

We need to stop agreeing with negative thoughts. Once you make it a habit to speak truth over yourself, negativity will no longer affect you— like water off a duck's back. It won't bother you because you're used to rejecting negativity, and constructive criticism will feel different. Instead of feeling attacked, you'll start asking, "Is there truth in what this person is saying? God, if so, show me so I can change." If there's no truth, it's your responsibility to reject it, preventing your mind from trapping you in a mental prison.

66

Without God, I would never have a story to tell. I am thankful He brought me through my darkest seasons and remained the source I could depend on most.

To my late mother, Monique Veasley, I am grateful to have been your daughter. Everything you prayed over me is coming to pass; even though you are no longer here, I know you left me with the most valuable treasure and key to life: the knowledge of coming to know Jesus Christ as my Lord and Savior. Your legacy lives on through every life you've touched, including mine.

99

A Note For You

Hey girl!

First of all, thank you for your support and for reading this book. I pray this book has been a blessing to you and has brought clarity, understanding, and a new perspective on your life. I pray you will take the time to heal, grow, and thrive into becoming the woman you are called to be. God has a great purpose for your life, and you must know you are worth it. I would love to connect with you and hear your thoughts, your testimony, and how this book has helped you. Share this with someone you know could benefit from reading.

Know that starting over is an opportunity for a new beginning. Becoming the woman you were created to be has always been a part of God's plan.

Princess Veasley

Here's how we can connect:

- hello@whosheis.com
- iamprincessveasley
- @princessveasley

A Gift For You!

Download the How to Heal From A Heartbreak Workbook as my free gift you by scanning the QR code or following the website below. ♀

https://princessveasley.com/resources

I want to hear from you!

If this book has blessed you, given you insight or has helped you in any way please let me know by leaving a review. Your feedback is greatly appreciated and will help others know if this book could help them too.

Ways you can leave a review:

1. If you purchased via Amazon, please leave a review under this book on Amazon.com

2. Leave your review by scanning the QR code or following the website below.

https://princessveasley.com/hervoice-review

About the Author

Princess Veasley is a dedicated mother of three, residing in the vibrant city of Dallas, Texas. Her personal journey of faith and self-discovery has shaped her into a passionate advocate for healing and spiritual growth. After navigating her own struggles with identity and self-worth in relationships, Princess realized the importance of understanding who she was in Christ and now works to help others do the same. Her mission is to guide women toward living a life of freedom, authenticity, and purpose without compromising their faith.

Through her writing, speaking engagements, and her popular YouTube channel, @princessveasley, Princess provides a platform for those seeking healing and clarity on their spiritual paths. As an entrepreneur, she also aids visionaries in fulfilling their God-given callings by offering expertise in administrative structure and strategic planning, helping others bring their visions to life and positively impact their communities.

Princess's book is an extension of her life's mission—to help women embrace their true identity, find their voice, and step into everything God has intended for them. Her work serves as a beacon of hope and inspiration, encouraging others to embark on their own healing journeys and realize their full potential in Christ.

www.ingramcontent.com/pod-product-compliance
Lightning Source LLC
Chambersburg PA
CBHW032027090426
42741CB00006B/754